Customs & Etiquette of
Italy

ABOUT THE AUTHOR

HUGH SHANKLAND has spent 40 years visiting Italy and
teaching the language, history and culture. He recently retired
as Principal Lecturer in Italian Studies at the University of
Durham, England.

ILLUSTRATED BY
IRENE SANDERSON

Customs & Etiquette of
ITALY

Hugh Shankland

Customs & Etiquette of Italy
by Hugh Shankland

First published 1991 by Global Books Ltd.
Second edition 1996, Third edition 2001
This edition published 2005 by
Simple Guides an imprint of Bravo Ltd.
59 Hutton Grove
London N12 8DS
Tel: +44 (0) 208 446 2440
Fax: +44 (0) 208 446 2441
Enquiries: sales@bravo.clara.net

© 2005 Bravo Ltd.

ISBN 1-85733-393-4

British Library Cataloguing in Publication Data
A CIP catalogue entry for this book
is available from the British Library

Cover image: ©Philip Craven / www.travel-ink.co.uk
Set in Futura 11 on 12 pt by Bookman, Hayes
Printed and bound in China

Contents

Map of Italy   *6*
Foreword   *7*

1 Attitude to Foreigners   *10*

2 The Spice of Life:
The Country, People & Climate   *19*

3 The Family, Men & Women   *32*

4 *La bella figura:* Dress & Style   *41*

5 Social Occasions & Situations   *47*

6 Communicating   *58*

7 Food & Drink   *70*

8 Out & About   *79*

9 Italy on Wheels   *87*

10 On Business   *92*

Further Reading   *99*

Facts About Italy   *101*

Index   *103*

Map of Italy

Foreword

Italy's best-known book on etiquette is called the *Galateo*. It was written 450 years ago at the height of the Renaissance by a worldly Florentine priest called Monsignor Della Casa, and was so successful that '*il galateo*' is still the Italian term for the norms of correct bahaviour. Much of the appeal of his affable little advice book on social graces lies in its amusing catalogue of 'don'ts'. For example, if you must yawn don't open your mouth and bray like a donkey, particularly right in the face of someone telling you their life story. Don't walk off after dinner with a toothpick stuck between your teeth like a bird making its nest. After blowing your nose don't open out your handkerchief and inspect the contents as though pearls and rubies had spilled out of your skull. Who can quarrel with that? And the *Galateos*'s golden maxim is still as true as ever: 'Good manners depend on consideration of other people's wishes rather than your own pleasure.'

Della Casa was writing at a time when the sophisticated life of Italy's courts and patrician houses dictated the fashion for the rest of Europe, and foreign visitors used to cite the Italians' invention of the fork as the ultimate in refinement, when until then all the world had made do with fingers. Today, what constitutes good form is more or less standard throughout the Western world, a watered-down version of middle-class conventions that prevailed when even Mussolini wore a bowler hat.

So this Simple Guide to the currrent '*galateo*' and everyday social relations in contemporary Italy will not presume to lecture you on such matters as how to hold your fork in the land of pasta, though admittedly eating spaghetti without getting a chinful of sauce is a challenge if you choose to obey the Italian don'ts (don't cut it up, don't use a spoon). It just sets out to provide basic information and advice for anyone who is interested not simply in visiting an astoundingly beautiful country but who is also looking forward to enjoying the company of Italians and getting to know the way they choose to live.

The days may be gone when well-heeled Northern Europeans and Americans regarded a stay in Italy as a kind of obligatory finishing school for any half-way cultured young man or woman, and yet not a few visitors still discover that the Italians still have some secrets to pass on to others about the art of living.

'You can never be bored in Italy!' (*In Italia non ci si annoia mai!*), a dapper eighty-year-old suddenly exclaimed last time we were in his country. My wife and I had never heard his extravagant claim before, yet it struck us as simply true. A complete stranger, he had insisted on showing us the superb paintings and stucco decorations made by local craftsmen long ago in his village church high in the mountains of Lombardy. To embellish his claim he entertained us to a colourful sample of Italian dialects, his booming varying voices filling the church, concluding with innumerable ways of saying 'boy' and 'girl' in different areas of the country.

Among the new material in this expanded version of a text first published in 1991 (with a revised edition in 1996) is a chapter called 'Communicating'. Not only that section but all these pages are an invitation not merely to observe the rich spectacle of Italian life but to share in the pleasure of discovering how difficult it is to be bored in the company of Italians.

H.S.

1

Attitude to Foreigners

Venice

Italians are used to foreigners: pilgrims, poets, merchants, artists, 'grand tour' travellers and invading armies in the past – armies of tourists today. Eight million people visit Venice every year, and there are only 75,000 Venetians. Being one among those eight million can make you feel no more than an anonymous addition to the statistics of the tourist trade, and at times you will not be mistaken if you choose to interpret some unexpected courtesy towards you as just another routine aspect of the nation's most lucrative industry.

On the other hand, such long familiarity with the presence of so many people from other countries means that over the centuries the Italians came to be uncommonly tolerant of outsiders. Also there are very positive reasons for this general openness towards strangers. Hospitality is an ancient Mediterranean duty – a section of the lowest pit of Dante's Hell is reserved for betrayers of their guests – a tradition far from extinct even in the much accelerated pace of society today. *Tutto il mondo è paese*, 'the whole world is one country', is a commonly heard remark when you begin to establish contact. In other words, for better or worse we are all human though we may call ourselves strangers.

Many Italians have connections all over the world, not only through international trade and business contacts, but with their own kin, relatives and their descendants among the millions who felt driven to emigrate in times when in so many parts of Italy it was hard to make a decent living. Those times are over now. Today, Italy is one of the wealthiest countries in the world, and in its turn attracts thousands of economic migrants from the neighbouring Balkan countries, and from North Africa and Asia.

Sadly, these needy peoples have not been so benevolently received as the traditional fairly well-off white-skinned tourists. Thoughtless or downright racist remarks are all too often heard from the most decent-seeming people. As in other affluent European countries which have attracted large numbers from outside, anti-immigrant feelings are fanned by populist politicians. One or two leading churchmen have even issued alarmist warnings about a supposed Muslim threat to Catholic values. These latter-day crusaders have their following, but the reality is that Catholic-inspired organizations are prominent in support of the newcomers and an outburst of violence against immigrants can bring thousands of people into the streets in support of a multi-ethnic society. In any case, almost everyone recognizes that these willing workers hungry for jobs you could not pay an Italian to do are here to stay.

Considering its exceptionally low birthrate, United Nations experts estimate that Italy would need 300,000 immigrants a year just to maintain the present labour force. A sociologist has spoken rather ambiguously of 'useful invaders'. If you hear talk of another 'barbarian' invasion, you can always point out that this one is more peaceable and productive than those of the Goths and Vandals.

These uncomfortable realities simply mean that Italy is not a museum but a modern country in continuing evolution. Rather than the land of immortal art and unspoilt nature projected by tourist brochures and sentimental films, it can strike the visitor as a very young nation that is only just outgrowing its pioneering phase. In no more than fifty years the majority of the population have come from an underdeveloped agricultural economy and small-town way of life to experience all the blessings and not a few of the drawbacks of newly affluent societies: conspicuous wealth alongside poverty and slums, vastly improved living standards for most people but polluted rivers and seas and cities, corrupt and inefficient government, high crime rate, sensationalist television, readily available drugs and porno.

In jaded moments one may reach the despairing conclusion that a gentle and almost virgin country has been irredeemably violated by indiscriminate modernization driven by a get-rich-quick mentality blinded by consumer dreams. But there is abundant evidence that the superficial gloss has begun to tarnish, and everywhere one encounters nostalgia for the good old days and ways. And here of course the interests of inhabitant and visitor coincide: can Italy remain one of those ideal spaces where the genuine comforts of modern life can be enjoyed without jettisoning all the profounder wisdoms of the past?

Despite these necessary reservations, the lasting impression of anyone who spends any time in Italy is that Italians like other people, and that they like to be liked. You will not need to go off the beaten track to find genuine warmth and disinterested attention. Visitors are frequently overwhelmed by the kindness they receive, often from those who can least afford it. An old proverb of the Italian South says: 'A man doesn't go out to work his land when there's a festa, or bad weather, or friends in his home.'

. . . the table is still the altar. . .

The Table – A Celebration of Human Fellowship

Even in these days of convenience food and super-markets, the table is still the altar where delight in human fellowship is celebrated. Bread and wine, a plate of pasta, spiced sausage and a fresh-sliced tomatoe, a cup of strong coffee: the plainest meal in good company can acquire the flavour of a ritual, good-natured communion in the name of friendship and the simple miracle of being alive together to taste this moment.

A chance meeting with an acquaintance swiftly progresses to 'Shall we have something?' (*Prendiamo qualcosa?*). On you walk to the nearest bar, not to get tight but to mark the occasion with a little ceremony. And do not presume, by the way, that you will be allowed to pay for the Martinis or the two little espresso coffees. 'You can pay when I come to your country', is the most that might be conceded.

'Prendiamo qualcosa?'

Spontaneous affability and agreeable informality characterize most Italians' direct dealings with outsiders. The popular image of Italian men as slavish attenders on women is quite fallacious. There is little pointless gallantry: men do not feel obliged to open and shut doors for women getting in and out of cars for instance. Such formality as you do encounter is more likely intended to put you at your ease. Communication counts so much more than form, and most people are quick to pick up on others' feelings and respond accordingly.

Language barriers are not felt to be a formidable deterrent to meaningful communication, more a challenge to draw on one's own supply of imagination and invention to make anyone uncomfortable feel at home, even if 'home' is only a train compartment or a restaurant. Admittedly, you may meet with a very different experience if you come up against officialdom, but that is because not a few officials see the kind of formalities they handle as a test designed to try the patience of the people they are employed to serve. In such situations deference is a one-sided affair, only expected from you.

'Diplomatic Immunity'

Non-Italians do seem to enjoy a kind of unofficial diplomatic immunity, at least in the case of infringements such as minor traffic offences. If stopped by the very intimidating-looking traffic police you will probably be subjected to the routine of producing your papers for scrutiny, but you are unlikely to be fined. One thing that makes an official all-powerful in his little kingdom is the excercise of 'discretion'.

The English-speaking visitor has an extra bonus. English has never been more popular, even chic. In one evening you can get your hair done at a 'Hairdresser' rather than a 'parrucchiere', eat at a 'Quick Service Restaurant', then meet friends in an 'Irish pub'. Not much familiarity with the language is needed to catch the drift of these opening lines of a newspaper article: 'Sono belle, super sexy e glamour: in hot-pant ballano infaticabili

nelle
are
spec
in E
reg
'roc
am
eve
ad

S
So
c
fe
n
are
today. Graffiti such as 'I love Man   e is
magic' testify to the universal appeal of English
among the young who keenly follow the American
and British pop scenes.

A word of warning is necessary, however, in
case it may seem you can always get by in
English. You will soon notice that people of all ages
say 'Okay'. Even sooner you will discover this
does not mean most Italians speak fluent English.
Far from it. Just like the rest of us, the majority find a
foreign language a rather tough nut to crack, even
when studied for years in school. What is agreeable is that nearly everyone is willing to have a go,
if only to help out, or as a welcome pretext for a
first conversational exchange.

Graffiti

Join in – Learn Some Italian

If it's nice to know your own language is so appreciated, why not return the compliment? After all, it is simple etiquette to learn to use a few words in the language of any country that is host to you. There is no need to feel shy, it is not a very Italian trait, in fact probably the most fundamental social assumption in Italy is that everyone wants to join in. For this reason Italian words occur throughout the text. Some pratical help in communicating is offered in chapter six.

2

The Spice of Life: The Country, People & Climate

'There are twenty regions in Italy'

There are twenty regions in Italy. This is an administrative convenience, but also a reasonably accurate reflection of historical and cultural differences between each one of these regions. As a single nation, Italy only came into being at the will of a minority of politicians and patriots in the decade 1860-70, little more than five generations ago. Until then, most of today's regions were separate pieces in a jigsaw of kingdoms and duchies and city-states running from the Alps to Sicily.

Many Identities

If, today, a southerner strikes you as more ceremonial in speech and manner than his central or northern Italian counterpart this is partly because for over a thousand years the south, from Sicily to Naples, was influenced by the code of honour and elaborate etiquette of its Arab or Spanish rulers. If the paintings of the Florentine Renaissance look radically different from those of the same period in Venice this is just a clear reflection of the fact that Florence and Venice had quite independent histories, each resulting in a different sense of identity and contrasting philosophies of life.

With the significant exception of Piedmont in the north-west (the Kingdom of Savoy, under which the whole country eventually united) and the territory of the Church of Rome more or less in the centre of the peninsula, most of these states eventually succumbed to foreign rule. Yet each preserved its own distinct government and customs and vernacular. Centuries of wars and trade barriers fanned animosity between neighbouring Italians, and reinforced local loyalties.

In attempting to weld these disparate entities into a single unified kingdom, Italy's early rulers created a heavily centralized state that was tailor-made for the nationalist dictator Mussolini to manipulate fifty years later. This over-centralized system run from Rome survived fascism's downfall and the passing of the discredited monarchy. But it saddled the fledgling republic born out of the catastrophe of war with a huge and hugely inefficient bureaucracy, and antequated mechanisms for decision-making that still handicap the smooth running of the country.

For almost the whole of the second half of the twentieth century the state was administered by an increasingly corrupt Christian Democrat-Liberal-Socialist coalition. Endless power struggles inside the coalition caused governments to collapse and reconstitute themselves with notorious rapidity, but the 'regime' itself was assumed to be a fixture forever. Since it was a powerful source of patronage its excesses remained tolerated and unchecked until the early 1990s when scandalous revelations of boundless graft at all levels of politics and big business caused it to wither away almost overnight. To Italians its passing seemed as momentous as the disintegration of the Soviet empire.

The 1994 elections, held after major electoral reforms, were a fight between the old established opposition parties and a cluster of newcomers: the ex-Communists with their allies versus a hastily assembled right-wing bloc consisting of the reformed neo-Fascists, a rapidly growing northern separatist party, and Silvio Berlusconi's Forza Italia party created from nothing in a few weeks and riding to victory on wild promises of a million new jobs. For fifty years the old regime had ensured that the opposing political extremes, Communists and Fascists, were excluded from the party (!) that was national government. The Communists, the second largest and the most effectively organized party in the country, were kept out because of the Cold War suspicion of Marxism; the neo-Fascists were shunned because their admiration for the glory years of Mussolini was too embarassing.

Politics may be confrontational and occasionally even murderous at street level in Italy, but in the end it is always about the art of accommodation. Now the old extremes have changed their images and even names and are both respectably mainstream. The ex-Communists, now social democrats, are the leading players in the centre-left coalition that has governed the country since 1996, presiding efficiently over the stringent fiscal reforms that enabled Italy to qualify for entry to the European Monetary Union in January 1999.

Polarization between left and right appears as strong as ever in Italy, but the hope must be that the country is finally settling into an era of responsible and efficient government based on the democratic alternation in office of two major political blocs: centre-left and centre-right. Coalition is still a necessity, since apart from the extraordinary profusion of competing ideologies in Italian political life, when two strong personalities within the same party clash over who is boss the loser will often invent yet another party.

Participants in these old-style manoeuvrings have to acknowledge that today television is king. The centre-right bloc is dominated by the charismatic figure of Silvio Berlusconi whose business interests include ownership of about half the TV and publishing industry, and a top football team, AC Milan. Despite (and also because of!) extensive charges of corruption and tax scams, this self-made billionaire calling for greater deregulation and big tax cuts is the hero of many of Italy's army of small businessmen and entrepreneours, not to mention soccer fans and TV addicts.

PRIDE AND PREJUDICE

North-South differences and tensions are found in many countries, but in Italy they are unusually strong. No area of comparable size in Europe is wealthier than northern Italy. In general, its inhabitants regard themselves as hard-working and law-abiding like their northern European neighbours and (in their opinion) unlike their southern cousins. The oft-heard complacent quip that 'Africa' begins south of Rome (even in the capital itself) has been current in the north ever since unification. But since the sensational revelations about the level of corruption among the Rome-based political class, dominated by southerners, the old prejudice has gained a vociferous public platform in a powerful northern separatist party called *Lega Nord* (Northern League). 'Thieving Rome' ('*Roma ladrona*') is its most potent chant, conjuring up a picture of greedy politicians taxing the wealth of hard-working northerners to squander on themselves or in hand-outs to millions of supposedly workshy southerners in exchange for votes. Laid-back Romans, besides pointing out that the corruption scandal actually broke in 'clean' Milan, like to taunt that Romans still have slaves: the Milanese!

In order to defuse the Northern League's clamour for the break-up of united Italy, the other major political forces are bound to grant much more significant financial and executive independence to the regions. But this could make the economically strong north and centre still richer, and the south yet poorer.

'*palio*' of Sienna

But regional pride and prejudice is by no means confined only to northern Italy. Despite the great social shake-up caused by the postwar 'economic miracle' which saw almost a third of the entire population relocate in search of work and better living conditions, the average Italian still tends to identify more strongly with his home region or even home village than with 'Italy', unless he is thinking of the national football team. Even then he will follow the fortunes of his own club even more passionately than the vicissitudes of the national team. In his view, genuine Italy and 'the best Italians' are found in his own small area of the nation: *La Nazione* is a daily paper serving only Tuscans!

Southerners resent the northerners' presumption of superiority, declaring them cold and stuffy, and champion what they see as their own much greater capacity for human warmth and '*simpatia*'. Of course those in the geographical centre, in first place the Tuscans, feel far superior to both the top and bottom of the peninsula, certain their way of life combines the best of both worlds, a perfect balance between northern 'order' and more 'easy-going' southern ways.

The Italian term for this sort of micro-chauvinism is '*campanilismo*', blind attachment to one's own bell-tower or '*campanile*'. It is reinforced by the survival of strong linguistic differences: most people have a pronounced regional accent which makes their provenance easy to identify, and over half the population is still bilingual, i.e. fluent in a local dialect as well. The kind of Italian spoken in

Piedmont sounds more than a bit like French, and nobody in mainland Italy understands the way they speak on the island of Sardinia. Outstanding elements of these local cultures may eventually become absorbed into the national culture, notably the popular songs of Naples and the literature of the Tuscans and Sicilians.

Real social and economic disparities do undeniably persist betwen north and south (where unemployment is consistently twice the national average) but equally one often encounters a wilful failure to acknowledge the enormous material progress of the southern third of the country over the past half century. A modern communications system and vast improvements in the overall standard of living and levels of health and education mean that there are now far less pronounced differences in the lifestyle of one Italian and the next, wherever they chance to live.

But this intense localism also has a very positive side. It is the passion which keeps alive age-old traditions and festas and assures that no amount of tourist promotion can turn genuine popular participation in events such as the 'palio' of Siena (a medieval-style horse race round the main square), or the 'regata storica' (costume regatta) of Venice into a soulless charade. It also guarantees the survival of a flourishing and wonderfully varied regional cuisine. Italians, who tend to look on a meal out as more an adventure than a convenience, will travel far to search out authentic local dishes.

Variety Fare: Wines and Pasta

Italy's rich regional diversity and localism explain why there are over 2,000 different names for a bewildering variety of pasta shapes, or why the country produces more brands of wine – at least 4,000 – than anywhere else in the world.

Variety is literally the spice of life: black pepper and butter and rice are traditional staples in northern cooking, as opposed to hot red pepper and oil and pasta in the south. Scented truffle grated over your '*risotto*' in Piedmont, in Liguria a pasta sauce of crushed basil and pine nuts, of hare and tomatoe in Tuscany, or fresh-caught sardines in Sicily.

'a bewildering variety of pasta shapes'

CLIMATE

The climate, like the population and cuisine, is much more varied than is often assumed. Temperatures in northern Italy are on average four degrees cooler than in the south, because the country extends over ten degrees of latitude. Driving from top to toe you would travel about a thousand miles by the national motorway (*autostrada*) system, from the Brenner pass on the same latitude as Berne in Switzerland right down to southernmost Sicily on the same latitude as Tunis in North Africa. Despite its long coastline the country is very mountainous, only a quarter is lowland. The towering Alps and Dolomites fringe the whole of the northern frontier region, while the Apennine mountain range runs like a backbone down the length of the peninsula from the Gulf of Genoa to the Straits of Messina, with peaks covered in snow until early summer.

The inhabitants of Milan, in the great northern plain of the river Po, have to endure winters as cold as Copenhagen with the two airports registering as much as a hundred days of fog per year, yet summers in Milan are almost as hot as Naples, without the refreshing sea breezes. Turin, the other great northern city, is even chillier in winter but its position at the foot of the Alps gives it less torrid summer days.

Coastal areas are everywhere dry and hot in summer, but subject also to violent thunderstorms which can cause sudden drastic flooding. Inland cities such as Florence and Rome are delightful early in the year, but can be unpleasantly heavy and sticky in July and especially August, even at night.

Avoid August!

August is the crazy month in Italy and the worst time to visit unless all you crave is a deckchair in the sun. The whole country is on holiday apart from those servicing the holiday-makers.

This is no time to do business. Offices and factories and government departments are shut and all have fled to cool off at the seaside or in the hills and mountains.

The press conveys the epic scale of this annual mass evacuation by dubbing it 'l'esodo', the exodus. Historic towns erected centuries before the motor-car are for once a delight for the pedestrian, but it is less gratifying for the visitor to find most shops and restaurants closed and public transport unreliable.

Towards the end of the third week, after the 'ferragosto' national holiday (15 August) life returns to normal. Fierce cloudbursts break the long heat-wave and a sun-tanned population drifts back to its homes and jobs.

Spring and early summer and autumn are the best times for comfortable sight-seeing, though in Easter week major tourist centres like Rome and Florence and Venice are packed to capacity, and throughout April and May you can expect to share the sights and sites with crowds of Italian school-children on excursions. September and early October, when hotel rates and plane fares are cheaper, are often especially beautiful with clear fresh sunny days at the time of the grape harvest. October and November, the months of the olive harvest, have the heaviest rainfalls of the year, but all the winter months can be wet. This is the time for the winter sports enthusiast, the opera-goer, the Christmas shopper in Milan or Rome, the magic of Venice without the crowds, but before the end of February pink almond is blossoming in the extreme south.

Florence

One of the great delights of Italy is how much of life is lived outdoors, at least in the warm half of the year. All the larger towns have more or less permanent outdoor markets and every village has its lively market day.

The Italians may not be great walkers but the before-supper evening stroll, '*la passeggiata*', is a ritual more unmissable than Sunday morning mass. Young people in particular gather at this hour, and for whole families it is a pretext to put on best clothes and wander arm in arm through the main streets and squares, to see and be seen.

In summer, all theatres and opera houses and the majority of cinemas shut their doors. Entertainment moves outside, with open-air feasting and dancing, string quartets in palace courtyards, films under ther stars, rock concerts and opera in city parks and ancient amphitheatres. This is the season for a thousand local festas and festivals.

Wet summers do happen, even in Italy. Whatever time you go, pack a light waterproof at the very least, and good comfortable walking shoes.

'la passegiata'

3

The Family, Men & Women

Children in their white costumes for first communion

In this Catholic country that shares its capital with the Vatican City, large families are a thing of the past. Italy has one of the world's most long-lived populations but also its lowest birthrate, so that there are now three grandparents to every grand-child. In the reforming 1970s, at the height of the feminist movement and in the teeth of fierce opposition from the Church and other conservative forces, divorce and abortion were legalized by universal referendum. However, despite alarmist cries about a 'crisis of the family', the family is still Italy's most solid institution. Myriad small family businesses form the backbone of the nation's economy.

Though divorce is on the increase, its comparatively low rate (five times lower than the UK) suggests that preservation of the family unit is more important than marital compatibility or fidelity. Children (not only one's own) are even more idolized now that they are so relatively rare, and when small are expensively dressed as miniature adults. All the same, although welcome everywhere they are not specially catered for. Children's menus are unknown in restaurants other than American-style fast food outlets and nappy changing facilities are almost unheard of.

Despite generous state compensation for redundancy and early pension rights, welfare benefits are almost non-existent for the long-term unemployed. Family ties offer protection, a domestic safety net for weaker members. Elderly relatives tend to be actively included in the family support network rather than being left to fend for themselves in solitude. As they grow, most sons and daughters preserve good relations with their immediate family and are in no hurry to leave home. Of those under thirty, seventy per cent still live under the same roof as their parents, though this is partly explained by high youth unemployment and exorbitant rents in big cities.

Again, if youngsters choose to go on to higher studies, as almost half of them do, they tend to attend the nearest university and for the seven or eight years needed to complete a degree stay on at home which provides free board and lodging along with all the tender loving care. A part-time job in a bar or pizzeria will raise reasonable pocket money.

Such a supportive and protective upbringing seems to encourage self-confident and secure personalities, although, inevitably, 'mammismo' (mummy's boy syndrome) is common. Indeed, aggrieved wives complain of interfering mothers-in-law in forty per cent of Italy's divorce cases. I have no statistics for 'figli di papà', spoiled daddy's boys, but the over-indulgence of male heirs reminds one that not so long ago 'Figli maschi!' (Here's hoping for sons!) was a common toast in rural comunities.

Married women are still expected to fulfil their traditional roles of housewife, cook and long-term mamma, but are increasingly also expected to be wage-earners. The economic pressures of the consumer society have thus only partially liberated them from broom and stove, although strikingly progressive legislation has helped to ensure, at least in theory, that they are no longer regarded as man's inferiors. The typical Italian male notoriously used to categorize women as either madonnas or whores, mothers or mistresses. Such caveman attitudes still exist – where do they not? – but today's greater social and sexual freedoms mean that relations between men and women are much more humane and relaxed, especially among the young. Macho images and Latin lover stereotypes are more likely to be ridiculed than applauded.

Having said this, a foreign woman on her own can still have a tiresome time. The best way to avoid the feeling of being hunted is just to be yourself, be natural and open in the company of people who act in the same way, and simply ignore anyone who treats you any other way, no matter how insulted or infuriated you feel. As at home, most of this is just bravado, the need to preserve one's standing with the other lads.

Be Rude in Return!

If 'one of the lads' absolutely refuses to stop bothering you, you can forget your etiquette. Have a good shout at him using any language you like. Do not be afraid of a scene, you will find plenty of solidarity. 'Being rude in return is good manners,' as Dante said of his own behaviour towards a particularly obnoxious sinner in Hell.

In rural communities, particularly in the south, you may still find the traditional separation into male and female spheres, but all in all wives and daughters are no more possessively 'protected' by husbands and fathers than in any other advanced industrialized society.

The popular press often features articles about Italian males supposedly 'in crisis', fearful for their egos and fertility in the face of self-confident 'new women' high achievers. The threat does not yet seem too great: no more than eight per cent of the country's top people are female, according to a fairly recent survey. The strain for women trying successfully to balance both public and private roles seems born out by its finding that sixty-two per cent of these prominent females were single, and among those who were married seventy-four per cent had no children.

'. . . using any language. . .'

Recent coinages like *'il partner'* or *'la single'* (a mature woman in no hurry to get married) testify to changing times. Less people get married now and when they do they marry later, and yet matrimony is a booming business. A church wedding is still very much the done thing, and families can practically bankrupt themselves in their efforts to put on a spectacular show in expenditure on the costumes and reception. By tradition the bride's family should even set up the newly weds with a home. A common way of providing for this enormous expenditure is for parents to buy or build premises for themselves with space enough for the future extended family. Despite the appearance of almost reckless consumption, the Italians are in fact great savers, second only to the Japanese. Disposable income is invested in safe securities and high insurance protection for family members.

SIN AND ABSOLUTION

Church attendance has declined dramatically, yet eighty per cent of the population declare themselves to be believers. *Famiglia cristiana*, Christian Family, is the widest read magazine. Broadly Catholic attitudes, in particular the prioritizing of family interests, still count enormously. The benign outlook that assumes all are sinners but none of us beyond redemption might go some way towards explaining why man-made rules and regulations are so often more honoured in the breach than the observance. Not only the flesh is weak; no one is particularly shocked by peccadillos like tax evasion (officially estimated at ninety per cent of the self-employed) and house construction in contravention of building regulations (millions of dwellings). Governments regularly pardon such universal sins by decreeing mass amnesties in return for simple confession of wrongdoing and payment of a token fine.

No doubt, in the fullness of time, a similar blanket absolution will arrive for all those hundreds of prominent personalities suspected of corruption in the *'Mani pulite'* (Clean Hands) blitz on graft which in the 1990s made the leading crusading magistrate the most popular figure in Italy. Antonio Di Pietro made them wriggle, but few of the accused have done time behind bars. Forgiveness is built into the legal system itself, which offers even assassins lenient treatment if they recant and turn informer.

An impressive benefit of the *'pentiti'* (repentants) system is that it has enabled the authorities to recruit hundreds of self-confessed *mafiosi* to help them fight the mafia. The mafia itself thrives on a brutal parody of ancient and admirable southern virtues of family solidarity and loyalty to one's friends. But mafia intimidation and terror tactics are not the only explanation for the fact that whole swathes of southern Italy – Naples and its vast sprawling conurbation under the control of the *camorra*, and traditional mafia fiefdoms in and around Palermo and Catania in Sicily – have an uneasy relationship with the law.

TAKING CARE OF 'NUMBER ONE'

Italians are the first to acknowledge their own foibles, sometimes to the point of apparent despair. We have no sense of civic reponsibility, they will tell you, unlike the Germans and the Scandinavians, or the English. We are a Latin people, with us rules are made to be broken, individually and even nationally: our country has the worst record for non-implementation of European Union directives. A popular joke runs: God created Italy, the nearest thing to paradise on earth, and then – to be fair to the rest of the world – God created the Italians. But if you catch friends in such self-critical mood, just try asking if they'd prefer to be German, or English. . . . My favourite apology for the Italians came from someone who knows her people very well, a psychiatric nurse: *Non siamo cattivi, siamo fatti male.* We're not nasty, we're just made badly!

The friend I have just quoted comes from Naples, where *l'arte di arrangiarsi*, the 'art' of looking after one's own interests, is a persistent theme in popular literature and film. The moral justification is that it is all a question of survival, nobody will help you unless you help yourself, a mentality that is doubtless typical of communities everywhere on earth where the 'have-nots' far outnumber the 'haves'. Until recent times this was certainly the case in Italy where most town-dwellers could afford meat just once a week, and the millions of peasant families only at Christmas and Easter.

Six hundred and fifty years ago, a comic masterpiece explored the Italian make-up more convincingly than any work of contemporary sociology. Boccaccio's *Decameron* (c1350) is a compilation of one hundred stories told over ten days. Moralistic tales of selfless heroism take up just one day, while the other nine are mostly filled with tales about how society's disempowered majority (the low-born, the women, the wives) through the ingenious exercise of their native wit win out over their 'betters'. Exemplary stories, in crude modern Italian terms, of how the 'furbi' (the artful) will always outsmart the 'fessi' (the artless). Even the triumphs of unscrupulous knaves are related with a relish which would seem more appropriate to a criminal fraternity!

'The Italians are cynics', a close friend concludes, in a resigned moment. I would rather say that she and our many other Italian friends are healthy realists, and exceptionally good-natured too, precisely because they do not have too high expectations of human nature in general. And along with all the laughter, all the 'cynicism', no one can fail to appreciate how contagiously the Decameron, that quintesssentially Italian work, radiates delight in good company, good talk, good food, good love, good living.

4

La Bella Figura: Dress & Style

'la bella figura'

In a country which boasts so many of the world's leading fashion houses and where individuals can seem so assertive, it is perhaps surprising that Italians are not less conventional dressers. But at all levels *'la bella figura'*, i.e. looking good and above all making a good impression, is a high priority. To most Italians the idea of not caring a fig what one wears is not liberating but incomprehensible, unless only a pose.

There is much snobbery over turn-out. A Sunday cyclist, a first-time skier, a seven-year-old footballer, is not happy unless he is dressed like a champion and a small fortune has obviously been spent on his kit. In their time, Italy's punks were surely the most immaculate in Europe. Dress rivalry, under the anxious guidance of parents, can even begin at nursery school. Unless you were trained from such an early age there is no point in trying to compete too hard. The best you can reasonably hope to achieve is not to lose face, not cut a poor figure, *una brutta figura*. Italians claim they can spot non-Italians a mile off, not only by what they wear but how they wear it.

The fashion industry reaps colossal earnings from the general vanity. But despite the sensuous and sumptuous parades down the catwalks of Milan, most people spend their money on smart rather than showily modish gear. Even those with a strong penchant for self-display tend to opt for expensive but safe 'labels'. Unless madly partying in fashionable discos, what people actually choose to wear is closer to the 'classic' cool associated with Armani rather than the show-off flamboyance of Versace. TV audiences know it is not the chorus of bespangled half-naked girls who have the real style, it is the balding presenter in his double-breasted suit and toned shirt and tie.

True elegance lies in moderation, insisted the author of the *Galateo* (see page 7), castigating all excess. An even more influential Renaissance manual took the same line, explaining all the social subtleties of *la bella figura* long before the term was coined. Its aristocratic author, Baldassare Castiglione, called his famous handbook *Il cortigiano*, the Book of the Courtier, and it was quickly translated into other European languages. He describes a privileged circle of gentlemen and ladies leisurely discussing what gives refined individuals like themselves their *grazia*, their easy stylishness, that enviable ability to draw attention to oneself without seeming vulgar. How is it done? A few are endowed with an air of effortless superiority by God or nature, some can hope to acquire it by imitation, most will only make fools of themselves by attempting what is way beyond them. Castiglione's handsome young courtiers are acutely self-aware, and their society is a stage on which all perform. Often things seem no different in today's Italy. On the humbler stages of the consumer society there can only be a few trend-setters, others willingly submit to the advertisers' pressures to do what is expected.

Little more than thirty years ago the level of prosperity now enjoyed by the majority was only a dream for the bulk of the population, and in this sense almost all today's Italians are nouveaux riches. Possibly this helps to explain the high status of material possessions and the widespread uniformity. This novel affluence was not gained without hard work, and the first returns were invested for the general benefit of the family in solid things like a refrigerator or a utility car that could double as a van for everyday work. Later a surplus became available for luxury goods – the top status symbol is by common consent a red Ferrari. But long before this stage is reached appearance can become more important than substance: style and taste become what a person is judged by, or simply spending power and image ('*il look*'!)

Back in 1960, Fellini's great film *La dolce vita* poignantly caught the flavour of the change to modernity, people of all backgrounds cut adrift from simpler lives and more certain identities. Visit any little village in the Apennines and you will hear older people lament the passing of the sense of community they remember: life lived at close quarters in narrow streets where the evening's entertainment was to take a couple of chairs from the kitchen and sit outside your door and chat with neighbours across the alley. Sadly, those who express such sentiments now as often as not live in pretentious villas built well outside the old village, surrounded by high walls and protected from the rest of the world by bad-tempered dogs. Even inside their houses, '*il look*' seems to prevail over comfort.

STYLE MATTERS

In clothes styles the quality of the material is valued as much as the cut. Aside from the universal 'youthful' appeal of a T-shirt or polar-neck sweater under an expensive zip-front jacket, and of course sunglasses and a carefully cultivated tan, when men dress more formally they tend to affect what used to be considered a distinguished 'English' look: an immaculately tailored dark suit, a three-button navy blue blazer, even tweed jacket with corduroy trousers in the case of more intellectual types. Much care goes into the selection of shirt and tie, and fine shoes. Jackets soon come off in summer, which makes a handsome shirt even more of a must, and an impressive wristwatch.

Women generally go for a tastefully glamorous look, with careful attention to their hair and the styling of shoes and handbag. Tailored suits are favoured for formal and office wear. Silk and leather goods and garments are essential elements of the 'made in Italy' look, and are of high quality. Ornamentation is often conspicuous and fairly costly: gold earrings and bracelets and pearl necklaces are widely worn. Jeweller's shops abound. Despite a vociferous animal rights movement, women have no inhibitions about wearing real animal furs, indeed fur coats and wraps are extraordinarily popular, to be sighted even in the heat of a summer night.

As for more informal wear, a sporty-casual 'American' look prevails for both men and women, whether or not one ever wields a tennis racket or jogs round the block: padded ski jackets, colourful tracksuit bottoms, designer sweatshirts and trainers. Jeans and denims are worn universally, by all ages. On the beaches and in seaside towns in summer anything goes that will catch the eye, barring total nudity. Probably the most 'Italian' of all accessories is the ubiquitous '*zainetto*', a mini-knapsack strapped to the back, first donned in its 'day-glo' version by every child on its first day at school. Many seem to grow so attached to it that they cannot be without some version in later life.

Even if travelling in the hot months bring a light jacket or shawl or cardigan for the cool of the evening. Since people are so clothes-conscious, men as well as women receive compliments if they take the trouble to dress well. More than the fashion parades, the most enjoyable way to experience Italian inventiveness and delight in dressing up is to visit the great Venice carnival in the period leading up to Lent.

Dress Code for Church

The Church has finally relented on the question of women and clothing, or at least to the extent of no longer insisting that hair is covered. But men as well as women may still be barred from entering a church if wearing shorts or a top that leaves the shoulders bare.

5

Social Occasions & Situations

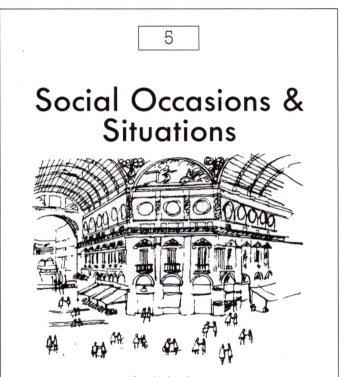

'If in doubt: shake'

When to shake hands? Always when introduced or introducing yourself, always
when taking your leave. So you could shake hands
with the same person twice in thirty seconds: if a
friend presents you to an acquaintance in the street
you shake hands immediately and again before
parting, even if not a word has passed between
you. Yes, that is ten times in the case of five

acquaintances! Since a handshake is a token of respect even more than politeness, it would be felt odd or offensive not to respond. In situations where people are well acquainted, shaking hands is more a mark of mutual regard: busy colleagues headed in opposite directions in the same corridor will momentarily clasp hands as they pass each other, scarcely dropping their speed.

If in Doubt: Shake!

Although at first it can feel quaintly formal, a firm handshake between good acquaintances is a warm expression of the pleasure of being in each other's company. If you are staying with a family, your hosts might extend a hand to you last thing at night and again next day when you meet for breakfast. So if in doubt: shake. It will never be wrong, and if the initiative comes from you it will give added pleasure.

When new arrivals enter the room in a fairly formal situation such as the start of a dinner party, even if they are well known to everyone all the men present will rise and shake hands. Women remain seated, unless an elderly or very special person has come in. A man might give a woman a kiss on the back of the hand, just a graceful compliment if done without affectation. Experts say the lips should not quite touch the skin!

'. . . a graceful compliment'

Two kisses, one on each cheek (commonly the left first then the right) is the norm between relatives and close friends when meeting or parting. Children, of course, are much kissed and hugged. People embrace freely, men as well. In fact men are seen walking arm in arm almost as much as women. It is good to renew contact. Friendship is precious, something worth demonstrating, even advertising.

What sort of things do people say? *'Piacere'* means 'Nice to meet you' when you are introduced. In fairly formal everyday situations, where we might say 'hello' or 'how do you do?', you just say *'buongiorno'* or *'buona sera'* ('good day' or 'good evening'). There is no 'good afternoon', so *'buona sera'* is used from about five o'clock on. *'Buongiorno'* is also a cheery greeting first thing in the morning between family or friends. '*Ciao*', meaning both 'hello' and 'goodbye', is normally used when you know a person quite well or in the company of children and young people; also when you feel on an equal footing with the other person, much like 'Hi!' and 'See you!' in English-speaking countries. '*Salve*' is an all-purpose greeting, felt to be less casual than '*ciao*'. It is becoming very popular, probably because between acquaintances on not particularly intimate terms it sounds neither too formal nor too off-hand (cf. 'Hi there!). '*Arrivederci*' is universally goodbye, though it, too, has a formal version which can sound rather stilted: '*arrivederla*'.

FORMAL & INFORMAL

All these distinctions between formal and informal are a reflection of a society that until fairly recently was quite hierarchical in structure and feeling – a century ago the formal mode was even used by children addressing their parents. Even now, despite the much more relaxed attitudes, anyone grappling with the language for the first time immediately comes up against the perplexing fact that there are two socially determined ways of saying 'you'. Language books instruct the learner that '*Lei*' is the formal mode of address, '*tu*' is the informal, as if that solved the problem rather than creating one. For how, in every situation, is an outsider in this culture able to judge precisely where the line falls between 'formal' and 'informal'? Will I sound over-familiar if I use the easy '*tu*' with this guy, or absurdly pompous if I use the grammatically complicated '*Lei*'? Can I circumvent 'you' until he uses one or other form, then take my cue from him? This is undoubtedly a useful tactic, but the fact is that although Italians can be quite sensitive about the issue among themselves, a beginner in the language will never give offence – any attempt to speak Italian is too much appreciated for that.

In any case, immediate recourse to '*tu*' is now becoming very widespread among even total strangers, particularly the younger generation, and not only in the south where '*Lei*' never really caught on. Italians of more or less equal standing who begin by using '*Lei*' soon reach a point where they feel uncomfortable with the convention, and so one or other proposes a switch to '*tu*'. Obviously, where status is unequal, this proposal (if made at all) has to come from the more senior figure... How much simpler seems our universal democratic English 'you', though it is worth recalling our own fumblings when taking the initiative to switch to first name terms. A good rule of thumb is to use '*Lei*' if in real doubt, but to launch straight into '*tu*' in circumstances where your instinct is to use '*ciao*' (see above!).

As for terms of address, even '*Signore*' and '*Signora/Signorina*' require some clarification, since they do not always have quite the same implications as 'Mister' 'Mrs' or 'Miss'. A girl or young single woman is '*Signorina*', but a mature woman is generally addressed as '*Signora*', whether or not she is married. '*Signore*', unless coupled with a man's name, is only used by a person in a service role, a waiter or a shop assistant for instance (cf. English '*Sir*').

In business and professional contexts there is much resort to titles: e.g. '*dottore*' (doctor, but also in theory anyone with a university degree), '*ingegnere*' (engineer), '*avvocato*' (lawyer or attorney), and '*professore*' (any teacher above elementary school level). Women professionals are similarly addressed: '*dottoressa*' '*professoressa*' etc., though the position has become confused by the feminists' claim that it is less discriminatory to refer to Angela or Isabella as '*la dottore*' or even '*la dottora*'. In cases such as whether to say '*la ministra*' or even '*il ministro*' (for a female cabinet minister!), you will hear both terms used in the same sentence, because no one is sure which is more politically correct! This universal respect for titles can sometimes seem truly excessive in the south where anyone with the smallest degree of social standing can expect to be honoured with at least '*dottore*'.

Titles of nobility were officially abolished fifty years ago when the royal family was banished from Italian soil after the creation of the Republic, but that does not seem to prevent the existence of a precise pecking order between Italy's hundreds of thriving principessas and contessas. The Republic rewards individual service to the state or industry with honorific titles like '*commendatore*' or '*cavaliere*'. '*Onorevole*' is a member of parliament, however dishonourable (200 were under criminal investigation in the early 1990s). The greatest conferer of titles is probably the owner of your local bar, as you will soon discover if, for instance, you let slip that you are an architect ('*architetto*') or an accountant ('*ragioniere*'). 'Titled' customers reflect so well on his establishment.

SUPERSTITIONS

In a country where plaster statues of the Madonna weep real tears and the annual decongealing of a dead saint's blood curbs the wrath of Mount Vesuvius, it is hardly surprising that Italians of all classes tend to be superstitious, at least to some extent. Fortune-tellers advertise widely and TV channels transmit daily horoscopes read by bearded and beaded astrologers or scantily clad female oracles. Many commonly held superstitions will already be familiar, others less so: a black cat crossing your path is a most sinister omen, never sleep in a bed with its foot facing the door, never put a hat on a bed, or break a mirror, avoid spilling salt or oil or pouring wine 'backwards' with your hand held under the bottle, and do not leave a loaf or breadroll upside down or the devil will dance on it.

Luckily, there is an instant remedy: make the devil's horns sign with your right hand (it is bad luck with the left!): jab your hand at the ground with forefinger and little finger projected, or better still touch metal (not wood) with the same two fingers. It will be a good year for you if the first person you see on New Year's morning is a man, a bad year if it is a woman. It must be progress that another version is now more generally accepted: it will bring good luck if the person you see is of the opposite sex to yourself.

As for other taboos, thirteen at table is definitely to be avoided; but many declare thirteen to be a lucky number for them, as it is for the lottery in Naples, and Naples is Italy's most superstitious city. Seventeen is the true unlucky number, and Tuesday or particularly Friday the seventeenth are very bad days. 'Neither on a Friday nor a Tuesday get married or start a journey', runs a very popular saying. And many add 'or do business', i.e. clinch a deal.

SMOKING

Smoking is likely to be more risky to you than any of the above perils. It is banned in all public places, including the subway, and *'vietato fumare'* (smoking forbidden) is one of the few injunctions that Italians almost invariably observe. Which is impressive, as large numbers are still quite heavy smokers. If you fall into the same category yourself, rest assured that it will be alright at the end of a meal to ask if anyone minds if you smoke. The odds are that half the table will light up gratefully. In restaurants you may be politely requested to put out a cigarette, although larger premises generally have a *'settore per fumatori'* (smokers' section).

GIFTS

When you receive an invitation it is normal to answer by telephone, partly because the mail can be pretty slow. It is customary to arrive with a bunch of flowers or a box of chocolates for your hostess, though flowers can be sent round in advance or delivered as a 'thank you' the next day. It is not the custom to bring along a bottle of wine, but when Italians do present wine the norm is two bottles of exceptional quality and generally with the same label.

As regards the old-time 'language of flowers', all that everyone agrees on these days is that red roses signify 'passion' and are sent in bunches of a dozen. Beyond that all is confusion, as some say yellow roses mean 'jealousy', others 'friendship'. Pink is safe. Gifts of flowers (except red roses) should be in odd numbers: five, seven, nine etc.

Twelve red roses

Never Give Chrysanthemums!

When buying flowers as a gift you must remember: never give chrysanthemums. In Italy they are the flowers of the dead; they belong on coffins and graves. For similar reasons, white lilies are never given to couples with children.

In the case of a meal among close friends or relatives someone will generally arrive bearing a beautifully packaged cake or tart from a local pastry-shop for dessert. Around Christmas no one would dream of calling without a large boxed 'panettone' or some other delicacy associated with the season. Extravagant presents of baskets and hampers of food and choice wine and spirits are given by companies and banks at Christmas or New Year to business associates and good clients. Other commercial 'homages ('omaggi') as they are known, include lavishly produced company calendars, cut glass, glossy coffee-table publications, inscribed pens etc. Easter eggs get bigger and gaudier by the year.

Every town has several shops that specialize in supplying the conventional gifts that go with big family occasions such as weddings, christenings, or first communion (for boys and girls around eight or nine, who are much feted in their smart white outfits). Each guest brings a suitable gift and is in turn presented with a souvenir 'bomboniera', i.e. a ceramic or glass bowl or sweet box containing sugared almonds, again in odd numbers, wrapped in white tulle. Anyone unable to attend receives the almonds through the post. Expenditure on the clothes and food is lavish. The celebratory feast can last all afternoon and is normally held in a large restaurant. Some families celebrate a name day ('*onomastico*', the saint's day corresponding to a person's own first name) in grander style than a birthday.

Obviously, in your case it would be appreciated if you give products and specialities from your own country as presents. For example, English china and Scottish woollens are very popular.

'*panettone*'

6

Communicating

'a little graphic sign language'

This chapter has only one purpose: to increase your enjoyment of being in the company of Italians by encouraging you to plunder the resources of your own language and any other expressive means you have in order to lower the so-called language barrier, even transforming its very existence into an extra source of delight. No one likes feeling lost and out of it, even maybe a bit stupid, when everyone around is effortlessly connecting in another language. But because Italians generally enjoy being together, they are very sensitive to anyone who is uncomfortable within the group and will make big efforts to relieve the tension and draw you in.

THE ART OF CONVERSATION

'*Conversazione*' originally meant associating with others, a condition in which it is natural to converse, as Italians still certainly seem to appreciate. Every town, large or small, has its central *piazza* which at any time of day is a place of 'conversation' for its townsfolk, particularly at the moment of the *passeggiata*, that magical hour around dusk, after the day's work and before supper (see p.30). You will see very few people on their own at this time, most will be chatting in groups of friends or family. *Stare insieme*, being in company, hanging out together, is unquestioningly felt to be one of life's most basic needs and pleasures. It gives everyone a chance to express themselves, and flare-ups are quickly defused. On Italy's beaches in summer, good neighbourliness and good humour prevail between the miles and miles of close-packed deckchairs and sunshades. TV chat shows are exceptionally popular and some can last for hours.

Where English does not get you very far, you should be delighted at the response if you try to connect in any bits and pieces of Italian you can muster. Genuine efforts will not be mocked, and mistakes will not be seized upon and pedantically corrected.

Aside from their normal courtesy, this is partly because so many Italians have had to go through the experience of acquiring 'good' Italian themselves. It is not the first tongue of over half the population who among their own kind speak a local dialect which in most cases is dramatically unlike the 'standard' language learned in school and heard in the media.

Sounding Italian

Italian is a particularly lovely language and luckily for the learner is pronounced more or less as it is written. You only need to bear in mind a few points in order not to seriously mispronounce a word. Consonants 'c' and 'g' are pronounced soft before 'e' and 'i': 'ce' as in 'chest,' 'ge' as in 'gentle,' 'ci' as in 'chill,' 'gi' as in 'gin.' On the other hand 'ch' and 'gh' are hard: 'ch' as in 'kilo' (Italian: 'chilo'), 'che' as in 'Kent,' 'ghi' as in 'give,' 'ghe' as in 'get.' 'sce' is pronounced as in 'shell' and 'sci' as in 'ship.' 'gn' is like the first 'n' in 'onion.' 'gl' sounds like the 'll' in 'million.'

In most words the stress falls on the next-to-last syllable, but if instead the last syllable carries the stress it is always indicated by an accent in written Italian. To help you further, in these pages a letter underlined shows where an unusual stress falls.

Fortunately, for the English speaker, both languages have a large stock of vocabulary with a common origin in Latin, so the meaning of a great many words is easily guessable. With most such words only small adjustments are needed to make the change from one language to the other, essentially in the way the word ends. Spend a few minutes studying the following list and comparing the examples in both languages and it should not be hard to convince yourself that you already possess a potentially immense Italian vocabulary.

ENGLISH ENDING	ITALIAN ENDING
-A	-A
idea, panorama	*idea, panorama*
-ABLE	-EVOLE
notable, favourable	*notevole, favorevole*
-AL	-ALE -ALO
special, sandal	*speciale, sandalo*
-AM(MME)	-AMMA
telegram, programme	*telegramma, programma*
-ANCE	-ANZA
fragrance, ambulance	*fragranza, ambulanza*
-ANT	-ANTE
elegant, deodorant	*elegante, deodorante*
-ARY	-ARE -ARIO
elementary, ordinary	*elementare, ordinario*
-ATE	-ATO
fortunate, immediate	*fortunato, immediato*
-CAL	-CO
typical, ecological	*tipico, ecologico*
-ECT	-ETTO
perfect, respect	*perfetto, rispetto*
-ENCE -ENCY	-ENZA
science, emergency	*scienza, emergenza*
-ENT	-ENTE
urgent, intelligent	*urgente, intelligente*

-IBLE	-IBILE
terrible, possible	*terribile, possibile*
-IC	-ICO -ICA
romantic, logic	*romantico, logica*
-ID	-IDO
placid, invalid	*placido, invalido*
-ILE	-ILE
fertile, automobile	*fertile, automobile*
-ISM	-ISMO
tourism, enthusiasm	*turismo, entusiasmo*
-IST	-ISTA
tourist, artist	*turista, artista*
-IVE	-IVO -IVA
active, initiative	*attivo, iniziativa*
-MENT	-MENTO
moment, element	*momento, elemento*
-ONY	-ONIO -ONIA
matrimony, harmony	*matrimonio, armonia*
-O	-O
radio, stereo	*radio, stereo*
-OR -OUR	-ORE
superior, colour	*superiore, colore*
-ORY	-ORIA
memory, history	*memoria, storia*
-OUS	-OSO
curious, scandalous	*curioso, scandaloso*
-PHY	-FIA
geography, philosophy	*geografia, filosofia*
-SION	-SIONE
version, decision	*versione, decisione*
-SIS	-ISI
crisis, analysis	*crisi, analisi*
-TION	-ZIONE
emotion, station	*emozione, stazione*

-TY	-TÀ
difficulty, quality	*difficoltà, qualità*
-URE	-URO -URA
future, temperature	*futuro, temperatura*

Do not expect the above patterns to apply in every case. 'Sentiment' is *sentimento*, but 'contentment' is not 'contentimento' (it is *contentezza*). Also, when an Italian word sounds like it must have the identical meaning in English this is not necessarily so. *Pavimento* means floor, *morbido* means soft. Still, the table works in hundreds and hundreds of cases, so don't hesitate to experiment.

Even if they do not fit into any of the above categories, you soon find that for various reasons a great many other Italian words easily stick in the memory, once you have met them. E.g. *lungo* (long), *difficile* (difficult), *numero* (number), *interesse* (interest), *strada* (street), *odore* (smell), *velocità* (speed).

A further help is the fact that many Italian verbs are more or less identical to the English. It is not too hard to guess what these mean: *abbandonare, adorare, arrivare, celebrare, continuare, decidere, divorziare, entrare, finanziare, flirtare, garantire, invitare, organizzare, preparare, privatizzare, sponsorizzare, studiare, visitare.*

The letters 'x' and 'y' in English are generally 's' and 'i' in Italain: *esperto, esistenza, stile, ritmo* (expert, existence, style, rhythm). The last example demonstrates that some English combinations of letters do not occur in Italian. For instance, there is no 'th' 'ph' 'pt' 'ct' 'bs'. Instead you find: *teatro* (theatre), *foto* (photo), *scultura* (sculpture), *fatto* (tact), *assurdo* (absurd).

An easy route to enlivening your participation in conversation is to assimilate some of the commonest exclamations. You will hear a lot of the following, and will soon get used to them.

Accidenti!	Damn!
Aiuto!	Help!
Andiamo!	Let's go!
Aspetta!	Wait!
Auguri!	Good luck!
Basta!	That's enough!
Bene	Good
Benissimo	Great!
Boh!	I haven't a clue!
Certo	Of course
Complimenti!	Congratulations!
Che casino!	What a mess!
Che importa?	So what?
Che roba!	Incredible!
Che schifo!	How disgusting!
D'accordo	Okay
Dai!	Come on!
Dipende	It depends
Finalmente!	At last!
Forse	Perhaps
Forza!	Go on!
Giusto!	Right!
In gamba!	All the best!
Macché!	No way!
Magari	Maybe. If only. . .

Mamma mia!	Wow!
Meno male	Just as well
Naturalmente	Of course
Non importa	It doesn't matter
Pazienza!	Never mind
Possibile?	Really?
Peccato!	What a pity!
Per carità!	God forbid!
Purtroppo	Unfortunately
Santo cielo!	Good heavens!
Smamma!	Beat it!
Stupendo	Fantastic
Su!	Hurry up!
Subito	Right away
Uffa!	Ugh!
Va bene	Alright.
Vattene!	Go away!

Could you get by in Italy with no words at all? The face and of course the hands, virtually the whole body, for most Italians are indispensable expressive resources, much as they were for Toscanini. Just watch people on their mobiles! So when lost for a word or expression there is no reason not to resort to a little graphic sign language yourself. Some Italians hardly gesture at all, while others' hands are never still.

Observe people in conversation and you will soon notice that each has his or her own idiosyncratic way of 'conducting' a conversation. One while speaking will seem to be endlessly kneading dough, another winding wool, another forever rattling an imaginary pinball machine, another tightening a lid or wringing out a wet cloth, another trying to fit a key into a lock just in front of his nose . . .

Some gestures are specific to a certain region, such as the South Italian 'no' (a tut of the tongue, with head jerked *upwards*), others are common to the whole nation, so it is not advisable to copy them until you are sure what they are all about, or when it may be appropriate to use them. Here are a few widely used gestures to recognize. I offer only one 'translation', but this kind of body-talk is actually capable of many shades of meaning.

- Dig a straight forefinger into your own cheek, then give it a half twist: **Fantastic!**
- Waggle a raised forefinger from side to side, palm outwards: **No way!.**
- Lay both forefingers horizontally side by side, pointing the same way: **They're close friends.**
- Point both forefingers straight at each other, then bump fingertips: **They're like cat and dog.**
- Lock forefingers, and pull tight: **They're hand in glove.**
- Clench the hand with thumb pressed against cheekbone, then draw down lower eyelid: **Smart guy!**
- Same gesture, but using forefinger: **Watch out!**
- Raise hands slackly in 'I surrender' pose, level with ears: **Search me!**
- Shake hand (even both hands) with the fingertips bunched against the thumbpad, palm up: **Are you crazy?**

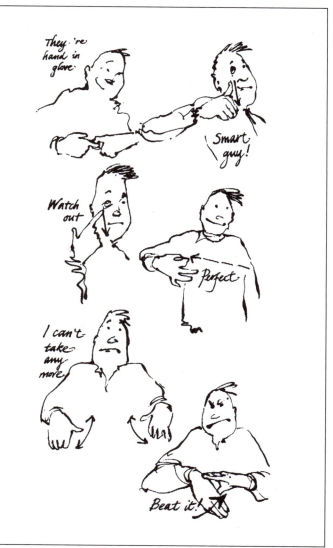

- ○ Hands lowered with fingertips interlaced, moved up and down: **Who are you kidding?**
- ○ Loosely shape forefinger and thumb like a revolver, and oscillate from wrist: **No such luckl**
- ○ Draw a horizontal line before your chest, with palm inward and forefinger and thumb pinched together: **Perfect!**
- ○ Cock both thumbs and shake your hands (turned inwards) vigorously from the wrist: **I can't take any more!**
- ○ With all fingers parallel drive your right hand hard between left thumb and forefinger a couple of times: **Beat it!**
- ○ For catching a waiter's attention you raise your hand with the thumb and next two fingers spread and then 'tremble' the hand from side to side. The word to call out is '*Senta!*'

ll gestures of course to be accompanied by an appropriate facial expression!

First Aid Grammar Kit

Italian has a very sophisticated grammar but is based on two simple principles:

1) everything is either masculine or feminine, e.g. *il giorno* (masculine: the day) *la sera* (feminine: the evening).

2) a verb changes its ending according to the message it has to convey, e.g. *parlare* (to speak) *parlo* (I speak) *parliamo* (we speak).

Some basic facts needed to apply the two principles:

1) The gender of a word is often indicated by its final vowel. This vowel changes to a different vowel to make the word plural:

a) Words ending in -O are masculine and change to -I for the plural (*il giorno: i giorni*)

b) Words ending in -A are feminine and change to -E for the plural (*la sera: le sere*)

c) Words ending in -E are either masculine or feminine, and change to -I for the plural (*il ristorante: i ristoranti; la televisione: le televisioni*)

2) The dictionary gives only the 'infinitive' form of a verb, e.g. *arrivare* (to arrive). To adapt it for other meanings, change the latter bit of the verb in these ways:

a) To say 'I arrive' use -O: *io arrivo*

b) To say 'we arrive' use -IAMO: *noi arriviamo*

c) To say 'you' (informal *tu*) use -I: *tu arrivi*

d) To say 'he' (*lui*) or 'she' (*lei*) or formal 'you' (*Lei*) use -A: *lui/lei/Lei arriva*

Nearly all verbs follow these patterns, but if the infinitive form ends in -ERE (e.g. *prendere*: to take) or -IRE (*partire*: to depart) then the (d) change is to -E: *lui/lei prende, lui/lei parte*. To express a negative put '*non*' before the verb: *non prendo zucchero*: I don't take sugar. Note that you do not need to say '*io*' ('I') since the verb ending conveys that sense already.

7

Food & Drink

'. . . at the dinner table . . .'

Breakfast ('*la prima colazione*' or simply '*la colazione*') is scarcely a meal at all. If you are staying in a hotel it is never included in the price of the room, and it is hardly worth the extra expense for just a pot of coffee and bread and jam. It is much more amusing to call at a lively local bar like half the rest of the population and order a delicious cappuccino and a '*pasta*' which in this case means pastry, a doughnut or a custard-filled croissant etc. Other popular choices are a toasted sandwich ('*un tost*'!) or a '*pizzetta*', pizza-bread filled with mozzarella cheese and ham or salami ('*salame*' to Italians).

Ordering a Coffee

As everyone knows, Italy has a great coffee culture. Note that for Italians one of its rules is that a cappuccino is only taken in the morning and absolutely never after a heavy meal. The choice is considerable, so in a bar you will be expected to specify:

un caffé	a small strong black 'espresso' coffee
un caffé ristretto	an even smaller stronger espresso
un caffé lungo	a 'long' espresso, i.e. weakened with more water
un caffé doppio	a double-size espresso
un caffé macchiato	an espresso 'stained' with just a drop of milk
un caffé corretto	an espresso 'corrected' with a drop of brandy
un caffé freddo	an iced coffee
un cappuccino, un cappuccio	an espresso with hot frothy milk
un caffellatte	an espresso with a lot of warmed milk, often served in a glass

Traditionally, the main meal of the day is lunch ('*il pranzo*'). The lunchtime break for most offices and businesses is two or three hours, so in many cases the whole family can be reunited. The children will be home, as school hours are generally only mornings, typically from 8.00 to 1.30, but including Saturdays. If you are invited home expect to eat with the children, and often with the television too, though no one will pay it much attention. Sunday lunch is often very special, with extra family and friends.

'In the middle of the day . . .'

The evening meal is '*la cena*' and begins about 8.00 pm. In families where a breadwinner cannot manage to get back home in the middle of the day this is the time for the big meal. Children in any case stay up late, with no fixed bedtimes.

A plentiful supply of bread (without butter) accompanies every meal, and there will invariably be wine on the table and bottled mineral water. If there are guests, the head of the household will pour the first round of wine and perhaps propose a personal or general toast ('*un brindisi*') and after that all look after themselves. When raising glasses the usual expression is

'*Salute!*' (Good health, i.e. Cheers!). Sometimes wine is not poured until after the pasta course. Italy produces some very choice wines, but generally no great fuss is made of the wine, which is just a natural accompaniment to any meal.

A full-scale '*pranzo*' is very substantial, but so varied and tasty that it validates the Italian adage 'the appetite grows with eating' ('*l'appetito vien mangiando*'). Most families would only treat themselves to it on a Sunday or when eating out. Two main course dishes are preceded by a starter, and followed by fruit, cheese and desert. The starter or '*antipasto*' might be an hors-d'oeuvre of cold meats and marinated vegetables for instance, or melon and Parma ham. In high class restaurants a selection of '*antipasti*' may arrive on a succession of different plates. The first main dish ('*il primo piatto*' or simply '*il primo*') will be pasta or '*risotto*' (rice dish) or a soup ('*minestra*'). The second main

Antipasto: a celeriac salad with Parma ham

dish ('*il secondo piatto*' or '*il secondo*') will be fish or meat, plus a cooked vegetable or salad as a side dish ('*il contorno*'). Generally not more than one vegetable is served, but often two or three varieties of meat – there are few vegetarians in Italy!

Potatoes do not automatically accompany meat or fish, though chips or fries ('*patatine*') can always be ordered in a restaurant. The side dish may arrive after the '*secondo*' has been consumed, salad being regarded as a palate-cleanser after richer food. Salads are usually served plain, and diners themselves add condiments to taste. Note that even for ordinary occasions pasta on its own (except perhaps in the case of '*lasagne*') is never considered a meal in itself, whereas a pizza is, and they come in all sizes. If you feel a whole pasta dish before the '*secondo*' will be too much for the children or yourself it is quite in order to ask for a half portion ('*una mezza porzione*') in a restaurant.

When costing a meal, note that as well as already charging VAT tax (*IVA*) on the food, a further amount may be levied for '*pane e coperto*', i.e. bread and cover charge, and a service charge ('*servizio*') will normally also be added to the bill.

Tipping

Service (10-15%) is automatically incorporated in restaurant bills, but since the waiter himself does not get it all it is normal to leave another 5% or so if you feel you have been well attended. In hotels, porters and doormen will expect a small gratuity, and the same goes for room service. Chambermaids should be handsomely tipped if you have stayed several days. Taxi drivers will expect 10% of the fare. In bars, more particularly in the south, it is common practice to present a small coin for the barman along with the tab for your drink.

EATING OUT

Italians eat out more than any other Europeans, so there are plenty of places to choose from. A *ristorante* is generally larger and more expensive than a *trattoria*, which is traditionally a family-run middle-priced restaurant with a limited menu but generally excellent food. A *taverna* or *osteria* should be even less pretentious. However, first consult the menu displayed outside, as there exist some very fashionable and pricey *trattorie, osterie* and *taverne*.

Apart from the growing number of McDonalds and burger joints which have an irresistible attraction for the young, for a reasonably priced meal the most popular choice with Italians is a *pizzeria*. Here there should be a big wood-burning oven and nearly as many varieties of pizza as there are ice cream flavours in a well-stocked *gelateria*. Pasta and other simple dishes will be on the menu too. For quick meals a *rosticceria* is a sort of high standard take-away, with spit-roasted meats and choice pre-cooked dishes. A *tavola calda* is a modest food bar. An *enoteca* (wine shop) or *vino e cucina* (wine and food) will offer basic but satisfying meals, the wine more than the food being the chief interest.

Cucina casalinga is a sign to look out for, promising good unfussy 'home cooking'. A *'menu turistico'* or *'prezzo fisso'* (set price meal) is generally not to be recommended unless you cannot afford better. With the recent arrival of many non-European immigrants other types of cuisine, notably Chinese and Indian, are becoming more widely available. Sushi is the new chic food.

DRINK

Whether eating out or in company at home, people linger long over the dinner table, with plenty of conversation accompanying the leisurely consumption of fruit and cheese (eaten with knife and fork, not on bread or savoury biscuits) and finally dessert (*'il dolce'*). As the meal draws to a close there is often animated debate about the marvellous meals everyone has enjoyed elsewhere, and various favourite dishes and how they should be prepared. It is not felt to be bad form in front of the cook! No *'pranzo'* would be complete without coffee, although many decline it after an evening meal claiming they do not sleep well after coffee. As a guest, at the end of the meal you may be offered a liqueur, grappa or sambuca, or an '*amaro*' or '*digestivo*', bitter-sweet aromatic syrupy concoctions that are meant to settle a full stomach.

Before sitting down to a good meal a vermouth or a chilled light wine such as Pinot or Verduzzo or Prosecco may be offered as an '*aperitivo*'. In the late evening brandy or grappa or whisky may be produced, but glasses will be infrequently filled. Few Italians are hard drinkers, as Monsignor della Casa was gratified to note as long ago as 1555: 'I thank God that for all the many other plagues that have come to us from beyond the Alps, this most pernicious custom of making game of drunkenness, and even admiring it, has not reached as far as this' (The *Galateo*).

'Al Banco' or 'Al Tavolo'?

First time visitors to Italy be warned: If you sit at a table ('*al tavolo*') in a bar with waiter service whether inside or out on the pavement the cost of a drink is up to three times higher than if taken standing ('*al banco*'). In the latter case, you generally pay for your order first at the cash desk ('*la cassa*') and present your receipt ('*scontrino*') to the barman specifying what you have paid for. In smaller family-run establishments it is more normal to pay after. However, there is one great advantage of the *al tavolo* option: once you have bought your drink you have acquired a pitch from which you will come under no pressure to move on. You can sit for hours writing postcards or just watching the world go by.

'. . . acquiring your pitch'

Alcohol consumption is high, one of the highest levels in Europe, but it is spread evenly among the population and most people's intake is confined to a couple of glasses of wine at mealtimes, even then very often diluted with water. As a rule, an Italian does not need to have a drink in his hand to feel comfortable at a party, or to down several cocktails before starting to feel 'good'. Partly for this reason older people shake their heads at the vogue among youngsters for driving hundreds of miles for all-night raves at fashionable discos where they can get high on Ecstasy or alcohol.

8

Out & About

'There is no queuing . . .'

Traffic conditions long ago reached crisis point in all the bigger cities, so consider taking the subway ('*la metropolitana*' or '*il metrò*') if stations are conveniently situated. There are networks in Milan, Rome, Genoa, Naples and Palermo, though only limited areas of the city and suburbs are covered. Public transport is cheap. An overall flat fare for bus or tram or metro is the norm and costs very little. Since your ticket is valid for more than an hour (e.g. 75 minutes in Milan and Rome, 90 minutes in Genoa) it can be used for more than one ride. Except in Rome, this also applies to transfer between bus and metro.

It is puzzling to find no ticket office at a metro station. Transport tickets are in fact sold at separate outlets, at news-stands along main routes and near metro stations, or at bar-tobacconists (look for the big 'T' sign for *tabacchi*). Tickets can be bought singly, or in a book of ten (*'un blocchetto'*). Day and weekly tickets are available, again at low cost.

Buses and trams are boarded at front or rear by the doors marked *'salita'*, the middle doors being solely for exit (*'uscita'*). Just inside is the yellow or orange machine where you should punch your ticket, although at times it may seem everyone else must have a valid season ticket or believes that only mugs do not take free rides. On buses seats are few, but do not expect a mamma to tell her bambino to surrender a seat to a footsore passenger ten times its age. In a crush, watch out for pickpockets, and like your fellow-passengers be prepared to call out *'Permesso!'* (Excuse me) and *'Scendo!'* (Let me off!) to clear a path to the exit.

When you take a taxi make sure the meter is running at the start of the journey. In southern cities there are many unofficial cabs and moonlighters. If you have to use one negotiate a (fair) price before you set out.

Elbow Power

There is no queuing for transport in Italy, a source of perennial irritation to the orderly British. Politeness will get you nowhere so be prepared to use your elbows a bit if there is a real crush, otherwise just go with the drift and you will be sucked into the vehicle like water down a drain. In other circumstances, such as in a bank or post office, where you find there is a scrum instead of a queue try to catch the employee's eye as soon as you can. He is the one who decides who gets served next, no matter when they arrived.

OPENING HOURS

Shops generally open at 8.30 or 9.00am, though food stores may open as early as 8.00, by which time markets are also doing lively business. Although the bigger chain stores and supermarkets stay open all day, the shutters come down on all other shops around 12.30 for a three-hour lunch and siesta break. In summer the opening hours for the latter part of the day are 4.00-8.00pm, 3.30-7.30pm in winter.

Despite the growth in mass-market stores, small family-run shops and speciality stores and boutiques fill the streets, another indication that Italians like things to be personalized. Nice to be greeted like an old friend when you step in, and to catch up on the gossip while being served by someone who knows your likes and dislikes. Remember at the weekend to do all your shopping on Saturday morning, as many shops observe half-day closing, and nothing at all will be open on

Sunday, except in the build-up to Christmas and in holiday resorts during the high season. Barbers and hairdressers close on Mondays. At least one twenty-four hour chemist (*'farmacia'*) will be open seven days a week in every sizeable town. (For business working hours see chapter 10.)

'alimentari'

Bargaining

Bargaining is the norm at markets other than food stalls. The convention is to offer half the asking price but expect to agree on something nearer two-thirds.

Smaller shops, particularly those near main markets, will often oblige if you are bold enough to ask for a discount (*'uno sconto'*). No one will think the worse of you, not even if a notice saying *'prezzi fissi'* (prices not negotiable) is displayed. Sales are advertised by eye-catching notices such as *'Saldi'*, *'Svendita'*, *'Sconto 50%'* , i.e.50 % off .

Banking hours can vary considerably and are best checked locally. Generally, all banks open mornings from 8.30 am to 1.30 pm, Monday to Friday only. Most open again mid-afternoon, but only for an hour or so, earlier in the north and centre of the country (e.g 2.30-3.30 pm), later in the south (e.g. 3.30-4.30 pm).

As with consulates and embassies, entering some banks can seem like penetrating a mini-Fort Knox, with a gun-toting guard outside and a bullet-proof glass chamber to pass through. But this is routine and everyone is very relaxed inside. However, as so often in Italy, more paper-work than necessary seems to accompany even the simplest transaction, and expect to be asked for an identifying '*documento*' such as passport or driving licence.

An extra complication is that the clerk you deal with does not issue cash. For this you report to the '*cassa*' (cashier's counter) along with your copy of the transaction and '*documento*'.

Fortunately, international credit cards now make life a lot easier, and cash dispensers ('*banco-mat*') are at last installed outside most banks. Most businesses used to be extremely wary of credit cards, but they are now accepted in all quality hotels and shops and restaurants and filling stations. If you need to change money out of banking hours, an exchange bureau ('*cambio*') will operate the same hours as shops, and they are located in all city centres as well as at main stations and airports. Hotels will always change travellers' cheques or foreign currency, though not necessarily at the most favourable rates.

Churches are Italy's free museums, as well as cool quiet refuges from the summer heat. Although they open early in the morning for first mass, they too lock their doors for most of the afternoon. Only the great cathedrals remain visitable all day. Museum opening hours also vary quite a bit. High-profile places such as the Vatican Museums or the Uffizi Gallery in Florence are open all day every day of the week and also have extended evening hours. But smaller museums may only open in the morning, and will almost certainly not open on Monday. The main archaeological sites are open all day, and close one hour before sunset. Bring a picnic to eat in the shade of a temple or a pine tree amid a ring of envious cats!

Cheap Picnic and Free Siesta

During those long breaks in the heat of the day, if you are footsore and a long way from your hotel you can always take a picnic and a siesta in a park, weather permitting. One of the ubiquitous 'alimentari' (grocery) shops will make up sandwiches ('panini') for you at no extra cost, and they sell bottled drinks and fruit. These small shopkeepers can be extraordinarily friendly and helpful.

When exploring a city on foot do not be too dismayed to find public toilets are few and far between. Almost every bar has one, and in Italy a bar is never far away. Standards of hygiene are usually tolerable. Do not feel shy about walking in and asking for *'il gabinetto'* or *'la toilette'*. You will not be expected to buy a drink or an ice cream in return for the favour, but no doubt it would be appreciated.

If you feel unwell a visit to the nearest *'farmacia'* (chemist's) could be sufficient, since a chemist is a highly qualified professional and many common drugs are available without prescription. *'Pronto soccorso'* (first aid) units are attached to most hospitals, and the service is free to everyone.

'Traffic can look daunting'

Traffic can look daunting, particularly when you find that cars will not stop if you wait patiently on the kerb at the appropriate crossing. No law obliges them to halt if there is nothing in front of them. They will stop or alter course when they see that otherwise they would hit a pedestrian, which is logical. So choose your moment well and step out boldly, making your intention plain. Since this is the system, drivers are used to responding quickly.

Some cities, notably Milan and Rome, have among the highest air pollution levels in Europe. Since a large proportion of city-dwellers have second homes in the countryside or on the coast, at weekends they flee 'lo smog' and 'lo stress' of their traffic-choked cities, jamming the exit routes with cars as though rehearsing for the great August mass exodus. For many the flight becomes permanent. Bologna, despite its reputation as one of the most liveable cities in Europe, has lost 100,000 people, a fifth of its inhabitants, in the past twenty years.

Since most bars and restaurants as well as shops shut on Sundays, city authorities find it relatively easy to impose occasional 'ecological Sundays', an entire day with no traffic allowed in the inner city. The experience is magical. The absence of the usual confusion and noise in the narrow streets and scenic squares is so eerie you feel you are walking in a postcard from a hundred years ago.

9

Italy on Wheels

'go native'

Drivers entering Italy from the relative peace of France or Switzerland can be dazed by the density and apparent chaos of the traffic. There is now one car for every two Italians and since most live clustered in high-rise apartment blocks their parked cars fill not only the roadsides but the pavements. The neutral term '*automobile*' exists, but all refer to their car as '*la macchina*', like a pet robot at one's beck and call. Florence is one of the worst places for traffic congestion, and in Rome cars would park on top of each other if they could.

Only watery Venice and the peaceful hilltowns of Tuscany and Umbria where motorists must leave their machines outside the city walls are havens for the pedestrian. Even though nearly all towns have instituted traffic-free zones in parts of their historic centres, this often only increases the pressure elsewhere.

For those with steady nerves, the easiest way to get around a larger city is to go native and hire a scooter. There is the exhilaration of movement when everything else is more or less at a standstill, you have accommodation for two, you can park it anywhere, and you do not even need a driving licence. Obey the law and wear a crash helmet for your safety, although many spurn it as a degrading curb on their freedom. Join the pack of other 'motorini' and you will also enjoy safety in numbers, weaving follow-my-leader through the cars and getting to be first off the mark at traffic lights! Bicycles can be rented too. But although cycling is a popular weekend sport, not many risk using bicycles for getting around except in the flatlands of the lower Po valley, in quiet provincial towns like Mantua and Ferrara.

First-time motorists in Italy return home with horror stories about narrow escapes from certain death. At least they lived to tell the tale. Speeding and risk-taking are the main causes of accidents, and mapcap youngsters heading home after all-night disco parties.

Road Signs to Note in Particular:

pericolo	danger
alt/avanti	stop/go
entrata/uscita	entrance/exit
rallentare	slow down
senso unico	one way street
deviazione	diversion
lavori in corso	roadworks
limite di velocità	speed limit
divieto di sorpasso	no passing
divieto di sosta	no parking
parcheggio	parking

At times you may feel all act like they are driving dodgems, but on the whole the Italian is a skilful driver. He (and she) may seem over-keen to prove it, but the intention is always to dodge not bump. Self-assertion is tempered by anxiety for the paintwork. In fact the accident rate is by no means the worst in Europe.

True, no one in Italy worries about speed limits unless they happen to spot a police patrol or a speed camera. And all too true, Monsignor Della Casa's golden maxim (see page 7) does not apply for Italians behind the wheel. As with queuing, 'me first' is the rule, and unless you want to risk causing an accident through your extreme courtesy or reverence for the highway code, you should join the crowd in the spirit of a rather better-known maxim: When in Rome. . . .

For the record, speed restrictions are 50 km (31 mph) in built-up areas, 90 km (56 mph) on the open road. On an *autostrada* (toll-paying motorway) the speed limit is variable: 110 km (69 mph) for vehicles under 1100cc, but 130 km (81 mph) for those over 1100 cc. On-the-spot fines for speeding are heavy. The *carabinieri* or *polizia stradale* (traffic police) can also fine you for not carrying all documents with you. You may be asked to produce: '*la patente, il libretto, l'assicurazione, la carta verde*' (driving licence, logbook, insurance, green card). An International Driving Permit is strongly recommended, as it will facilitate formalities if you have the misfortune to get into a scrape. All vehicles have to carry a red warning triangle, in case of breakdown.

When you fill up with *benzina* (petrol, gas) the choice is simply between leaded '*super*' or unleaded '*verde*' (green). Except on motorways, fuel is not readily available at all hours since most filling stations keep to the same schedule as shops, i.e. observe the long lunchbreak and close on Sundays. To plug the gap, a few automated self-paying pumps can be found in larger towns. Most petrol stations are not automated, but it is not necessary to tip the station personel who fill your tank for you.

In case of breakdown, the first words you need are '*autosoccorso*' (breakdown service) and '*autoservizio*', a garage that can cope with anything from a flat tyre to engine repairs. If you are anywhere near a telephone the number to dial is 116, which will summon the efficient Automobile Club d'Italia (ACI) to your rescue. The telephone emergency number for police, doctor and ambulance is 113.

Parking Problems

Statisticians calculate that an Italian motorist spends seven years of his life in a car, two of them spent searching for somewhere to park.

In cities, it is best to park your car wherever you can and proceed on foot or by public transport. Note that *zona rimozione* (or *rimozione forzata* with an appropriate picture) means that vehicles parked here may be towed away (and reclaimed at considerable cost).

Less obvious is that your vehicle will suffer the same fate if you leave it parked overnight where street-cleaning is designated for that night/early next morning. If in doubt, check with someone local. Adjacent areas of streets are cleaned once a week and every street affected has a sign stating the day and times of operation.

Never leave anything inside your car visible to a thief.

On Business

'Il made in Italy'

It can be a singular pleasure to do business in Italy. Contrary to ancient prejudices about unreliability and lack of punctuality and so on, you will find Italy's manufacturers and entrepreneurs and middlemen are very able practitioners of the skills of production and promotion, and well used to thinking internationally. '*Il made in Italy*' is how Italians term the combination of high quality product and design and export acumen which has been such a remarkable success story ever since the 'economic miracle' of the late 1950s, most notably in the case of the go-ahead family firm that typifies the Italian business scene.

But as the economy goes 'European' and 'global' many of these small and medium-size firms face stiff competion from bigger conglomerates with higher output and lower costs and more resources to spend on technological innovation. Other obstacles to business competiveness are long-standing low investment in research and development (only half that of France and Germany) and the lamentable inefficiency and inflexibility of public institutions. Against all this must be set the inventiveness and energy of the average Italian businessman.

Business can be a social pleasure too, as contacts will want to take time out to get to know their opposite numbers better, usually through the medium of fairly long and leisurely meals in excellent restaurants where relaxing together is not just part of the softening-up process. If this seems a waste of precious time during a short business trip, you will find it amply compensated by a willingness to work unusually long and flexible hours when under pressure. People in positions of responsibility can be on the premises as early as 7.00 am and still be around far into the evening. All the same, when planning a business trip you will need to take account of the normal Italian business hours and the shape of the working year.

Government offices only operate a half-day schedule: 8.30 or 9.00 am until 1.30 or 2.00 pm (convenient for the many thousands of state employees who augment their earnings by taking a better paid second job). Dealing with the sort of formalities that will take you to government or municipal offices can be a slow and trying experience, so start in as early as you can.

How to Cut Through the Red Tape

For anyone embarking on a longer stay in Italy, such apparently routine operations as procuring a 'permesso di soggiorno' (residence permit) from the police, or just opening a bank account or getting a telephone installed, can turn out to be anything but simple and straightforward.

To save time and hassle ask a local friend or colleague to come along to help smooth the way. In extreme cases follow their example and resort to the services of some recommended middleman who can work mysterious magic with bureaucrats. Just be happy to pay, without asking how he does it!

'the long Mediterranean lunchbreak'

Small and medium-size firms throughout the country still generally observe the long Mediterranean lunchbreak, working 9.00am to 1.00 pm, then from about 3.00 till 6.00 or 7.00 pm. Some are changing over to the international standard 9-5 office schedule (*'orario americano'*), but this is extremely rare in southern Italy.

National Holidays

Apart from Christmas Day and Boxing Day, New Year's Day, Easter Monday, and the universal summer vacation build-up to 15 August (*'ferragosto'* or the Feast of the Assumption), national holidays in the working calendar are:

6 January (Epiphany)
25 April (Liberation Day)
1 May (Labour Day)
2 June (Republic Day)
1 November (All Saints)
8 December (Immaculate Conception)

If on some other weekday no one answers your call this could be because the whole office has taken a *'ponte'*, a 'bridge' day off between a national holiday and *'il weekend'*. Another reason could be some purely local holiday to honour the patron saint of the town. For instance, few businesses will operate in Milan on 7 December, the feast of St Ambrose. Romans even get two annual local holidays, one Christian and one pagan: 29 June, the feastday of Rome's co-patrons Saints Peter and Paul, and 21 April, the traditional Roman 'birthday' commemorationg the city's foundation by Romulus.

Never in August

Remember that for at least the first three weeks of August virtually all businesses close down entirely, and government offices if open will only be manned by a skeleton staff. Moreover, the last days in July will be marked by a slowing down process in anticipation of the big August break. (see page 30)

Fax and e-mail facilities have been a great asset for Italian business efficiency, as the country's postal system though much improved is still relatively slow and not always reliable. To ensure quick and safe arrival even ordinary post is generally sent 'raccomandata' (registered) or 'espresso' (express). The priority mail ('posta prioritaria') service is only twice the cost of ordinary mail and guarantees delivery within 48 hours inside Italy. 'CAI Post' is a more costly public service promising 24-hour delivery to any destination within Europe. Main post offices open all day during the week, but close at 1.00 pm on Saturdays.

Even if initiating your side of the correspondence in English you can expect to receive replies in Italian from smaller firms. Commercial and bureaucratic Italian are terminologies all of their own, so it can be advisable to turn to a translation agency to decipher them.

On the other hand, in face-to-face negotiation you will have the advantage that English will be assumed to be the lingua franca. But since relatively few Italians are particularly confident in English they will probably avail themselves of at least the token presence of an interpreter or an English-speaking colleague.

As well as an air of professional expertise, the ability to appear relaxed and friendly will aid the reception of your point of view. Be open to exchanges on non-business matters, as Italians like to know you are a person too. Larger companies have their own bars and canteens on the premises, and a coffee or a shared bottle of beer will be part of the warm-up. Any effort at small talk in Italian should be well-received, and in any case anyone in the same field of operations as yourself should be very familiar with the relevant English technical jargon. On the more general level, you will find that many English or American terms particularly to do with technology, commerce, sport and the media are widely understood and are more and more part of the contemporary Italian vocabulary.

The classic Gambalonga

If you hope to impress personally, you can cut a *bella figura* yourself by investing in the much admired best quality English men's suits and shoes. For women, a smart dress sense is of course particularly appreciated.

Transport and airport workers' snap strikes are a hazard to travellers with little time on their hands, commonly staged when mass annual contracts are up for negotiation, or to threaten maximum disruption around the time of national holidays. For getting around the country, the fast Inter-City trains are very reliable and relatively inexpensive. The much-used internal flights are indispensable for the otherwise lengthy journeys between north and south. Note, however, that some airports (e.g. Milan, Rome, Venice) can be a long way out of town.

How to Use a Telephone

Unless you have your own mobile phone, making a call can be a little tricky. Note that you must always first dial the area code, even for a call within the same area you are in. Coin-operated phones only take small coins or equivalent tokens ('*gettoni*'), which means you have to feed in whole handfuls for long-distance calls. Better to buy a prepaid phone card ('*una carta telefonica*'), but note that it won't function unless you tear off the marked corner. Perhaps the most convenient system is the one found in many bars: a '*telefono a scatti*' which records the number of units for each call you make. The barman switches it on for you, and afterwards you pay him for the units used.

Further Reading

Innumerable books are available by outside observers but very few have been written by Italians themselves, from inside the culture. The classic account is Luigi Barzini's *The Italians*, first published in 1964, a shrewd and very entertaining dissection of his countrymen's virtues and foibles. A lively recent addition is Arturo Barone's refreshingly uninhibited and opinionated *Italians First!* Charles Richards's *The New Italians* is one among many useful reports by foreign journalists. But the most informative 'inside' look at contemporary Italy is William Ward's *Getting It Right in Italy*. A helpful practical guide for anyone embarking on a longer stay is Victoria Pybus and Rachael Robinson, *Live and Work in Italy*.

Chiantishire memoirs (and novels and cookbooks) written by second-home owners from Britain or America are now almost an industry. For all the honesty of their tales of the trials and tribulations of setting up home abroad, most view Italy through rose-tinted spectacles. A more caustic but convincing picture is found in Tim Parks's tales of everyday life in a north Italian family and neighbourhood: *Italian Neighbours* and *An Italian Education*.

From a southern perspective, try Luciano De Crescenzo's *Thus Spake Bellavista*, an affectionate portrait of the idiosyncracies of the author's fellow-Neapolitans. For the darker side of the south read Peter Robb's riveting *Midnight in Sicily*. Also the great Sicilian novel, *The Leopard* by Giuseppe Di Lampedusa. For a mouth-watering introduction to Italy's regional diversity, sample Claudia Roden's *The Food of Italy*. Finally, look out for any of the 'Aurelio Zen' thrillers by Michael Dibdin (*Ratking, Dead Lagoon, Blood Rain* etc) for gripping holiday reading as well as a valid impression of life from an Italian perspective.

The works of Italian literature mentioned in the text are: Giovanni Boccaccio, *The Decameron*; Baldassare Castiglione, *The Courtier*; Giovanni Della Casa, *The Galateo*. All titles in translation in the Penguin Classics series.

Facts About Italy

Ten years ago a UNESCO report made the claim that 60% of the planet's entire artistic, historical and archaeological heritage is concentrated in Italy, 30% of it in Rome. Recently restored supreme masterpieces of painting include Michelangelo's Sistine Chapel ceiling and 'Last Judgement' in the Vatican, Leonardo Da Vinci's 'Last Supper' in Milan, Piero Della Francesca's fresco cycle of the 'True Cross' in Arezzo, and Masaccio's frescos 'Stories of Saint Peter' in the Chiesa del Carmine, Florence.

Although often fondly called in Dante's phrase *il Bel Paese*, the Beautiful Country (also the name of a famous cheese), many areas of natural beauty have been ruined by indiscriminate 'development', particularly in coastal areas. At the last count, 170,000 new dwellings in Sicily had sprung up in contravention of building regulations which outlaw construction at a distance of less than 150 metres from the shoreline.

As if man's ravages were not enough, *il Bel Paese* is also exceptionally vulnerable to natural disasters: earthquakes, floods, landslips, forest fires. Over 200,000 people have died in earthquakes during the last hundred years, more than half of them in the terrible Messina earthquake of 1908. The worst recent earthquake (Irpinia, 1980) caused 2735 fatalities. Europe's only two active volcanoes are both in or near Sicily: mighty Mount Etna, and the remote volcanic island of Stromboli. Vesuvius, only just outside Naples, last erupted in 1944, but no vulcanologist believes that it was its final performance.

The population is almost 58 million but within the next fifty years it could fall to 52 million with the present low birthrate (half what it was thirty years ago) and curbs on immigration. Italian women still want to be mothers, but not *only* mothers. An unusually high proportion (88%) experience motherhood, but then over half decide not to have another child. This indicates a profound change in women's lifestyles and expectations. However, women still make up only 18% of the professional and technical workforce. A century ago their average life expectancy was 43 years, today it is 82.

The richest northern region, Lombardy (main city Milan) accounts for 20% of Italy's GDP. Average incomes in the poorest area, Calabria, the southernmost mainland region, are only half those of Lombardy. One third of the population of Calabria emigrated to Australia in the years after the Second World War.

Two mini-states lie within Italy's borders: Vatican City, the tiniest state in the world (108 acres), and San Marino (23 square miles), the world's oldest extant republic, dating from the fourth century AD.

The Colosseum in Rome held 50,000 spectators. Even now, on a summer's night in the Arena at Verona, a huge first-century amphitheatre in the centre of the city, you can join 25,000 spectators to watch sumptuously staged open-air operas by Verdi and Puccini. Nevertheless today's real amphitheatres are the great football stadiums, and the gladiators are called Baggio, Maldini, Di Piero, Totti. . .

Some of the best-preserved monuments of the civilization of ancient Greece are actually in southern Italy, known as Magna Graecia while it was a Greek colony. The most impressive temples are at Paestum (south of Naples) and at Selinunte, Agrigento and Segesta in Sicily. The Greek theatre at Syracuse is still the largest theatre in the world.

One of the most memorable ways of experiencing the layering of civilizations in Italy is to visit the church of San Clemente in Rome, overseen by friendly Irish Dominicans. The eleventh-century upper church contains a magnificent Romanesque mosaic, but also Renaissance wall paintings and lavish Baroque decor; under its floor you can visit a fourth-century church containing fragments of frescos, one of them with the oldest inscription in Italian; descending even further, thirty metres below street level, you find yourself in a narrow alley in ancient Rome leading to a first century patrician house and a Mithraic temple.

Index

abortion 32
AC Milan 23
address, terms of 50, 51
alcohol 78
Alps 20, 28
Apennine (range) 28, 44
Armani 42
Automobile Club d'Italia
(ACI) 90

Balkans 11
banking (hours) 83
bargaining 82
Berlusconi, Silvio 23
birthrate 32
Boccaccio 39
Bologna 86
breakdown (car) 90
business 92ff

Calabria 102
Castiglione, Baldassare 43
Catania 38
Catholic(s) 12, 32, 37
Christmas 30, 39, 56
Church (of Rome) 20, 32, 46
church(es) 36, 84
cinema 31
Cinque Terra 2
climate 28ff
coffee (ordering) 71
Communist(s) 21, 22
conversation 49ff, 59ff
credit cards 83
cycling 88

Da Vinci, Leonardo 101
Dante 11, 101
Decameron 39, 40

Della Casa, Monsignor 7, 8,
77, 89
Di Pietro, Antonio 38
dialects 9
divorce 32
Dolomites 28
dress 41, 42
drink 76ff

Easter (egg) 56
Easter 29, 39
eating out 75
English (language) 16, 17, 59
Etiquette 18, 35
Etna, Mount 101
European Monetary Union 22

family 32ff
Fascist(s) 22
fashion 42
Fellini 44
Ferrara 88
Ferrari 44
first aid 85
Florence 20, 28, 29, 84, 87
flowers (as gift) 55, 56
friendship 49

Galateo 7, 8, 42, 77
Genoa, Gulf of 28, 79
gestures 66
gifts 55
government 21, 37, 93, 96
graffiti 17
grammar 68

handshake 47, 48
holidays (national) 95

Il cortigiano 43

immigrants 12
Italian (language) 18, 60ff

kiss 49

La dolce vita 44
Latin 60
Lent 46
Liguria 27

Mafia 38
Magna Grecia 102
Manarola 2
Mantua 88
Marxism 22
Mass 30
McDonalds 75
meals 70ff
Mediterranean 11
Messina 101
Messina, Straits of 28
Michelangelo 101
migrants 11
Milan 17, 24, 28, 30, 42, 79, 86
monarchy 21
Mussolini 21

Naples 20, 28, 38, 39, 54, 79, 101
New Year 56
North Africa 11
Northern League 24

opera house 31

Palermo 38, 79
parking 91
Pasta 27, 70, 73, 75
Piedmont 26, 27
pizza 70, 74, 75
Po, river 28
    valley 88
police 16
Puccini 102

queuing 81

Region 19
Renaissance 20, 102
road (signs) 89
Rome 23, 24, 28, 30, 79, 80, 86, 87, 89, 102

Sardinia 26
Savoy 20
shopping 30
shops 81, 82
Sicily 20, 27, 38, 101, 102
Siena 26
Sistine Chapel 101
smoking 54
Stromboli 101
style 41ff
superstition 53, 54

taxi (drivers) 75
telephone 98
theatre 31
tipping 75
titles 52
toilets (public) 84
traffic 79
transport (public) 79ff
Tuscans 25
Tuscany 27
TV 23, 42, 53, 59, 72

Uffizi Gallery 84
Umbria 88
United Nations 12

Vatican City 32
Vatican Museums 84
Vatican, the 101
Venice 10, 20, 26, 29, 30, 88
Verdi 102
Verona 102
Versace 42
Vesuvius, Mount 53, 101

wine 27, 72, 73, 78